Young Trailblazers

The Book of
Black Inventors and Scientists

Young Trailblazers

The Book of
Black Inventors and Scientists

By M.J. Fievre

Illustrations by Kim Balacuit

CORAL GABLES

Cover, illustration, and layout design: Kim Balacuit
Images used under license from Adobe Stock

For permission requests, please contact the publisher at:
Mango Publishing Group
2850 S Douglas Road, 2nd Floor
Coral Gables, FL 33134 USA
info@mango.bz

For special orders, quantity sales, course adoptions and corporate
sales, please email the publisher at sales@mango.bz. For trade
and wholesale sales, please contact Ingram Publisher Services at
customer.service@ingramcontent.com or +1.800.509.4887.

Young Trailblazers: The Book of Black Inventors and Scientists

Library of Congress Cataloging-in-Publication number: 2021934939
ISBN: (print) 978-1-64250-606-8 (ebook) 978-1-64250-607-5
BISAC category code JNF007050, JUVENILE NONFICTION / Biography &
Autobiography / Cultural, Ethnic & Regional

Printed in the United States of America

Contents

Introduction

Becoming a Black scientist or inventor was next to impossible for many years because of laws that kept Black people and white people separate, and because enslaved Blacks were not allowed to read or write.

This book is filled with people who didn't let anything stop them on their quests to becoming trailblazers in invention or science. Their stories are here to show you that nothing can stop you if you work hard and have faith in yourself, and to teach you all about the marvelous world of Black science and invention.

Along with their life stories, you'll find interesting facts, words you should know, and quotations from these Black trailblazers in science and invention. Maybe you'll find someone who inspires you to make a difference in the world!

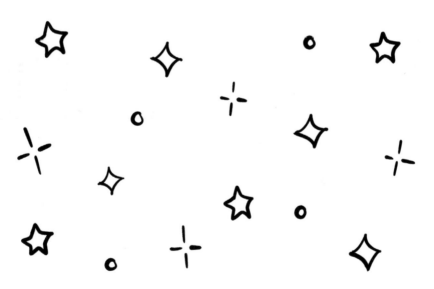

Alexa Canady

"...somewhere in your life there has to be a passion. There has to be some desire to go forward. If not, why live?"

Dr. **Alexa Canady** is the first Black American woman to become a **neurosurgeon**. A neurosurgeon is a doctor who performs operations on people's brains. She was born in **Lansing, Michigan**, in 1951. She and her younger brother were the only two Black children in their entire school. It was very hard for her because she faced a lot of discrimination during her school years. One time, a teacher even switched her test grades with those of a white student to hide how smart young Alexa really was! But her parents taught her the importance of education, and she worked hard to overcome hardships and do well in school.

She graduated with honors from her high school and went to the University of Michigan. At first, she majored in mathematics, but she did not love her math classes and almost dropped out of college! She then discovered that she loved **zoology**, the study of animals. After she got her bachelor's degree, Alexa learned that not many Black people were studying medicine,

Words You Should Know

» **Neurosurgeon**: A neurosurgeon is a doctor who performs operations on people's brains. They treat people with brain diseases and brain injuries.

» **Zoology**: Zoology is the study of animals. A zoologist is a scientist who studies animals, how they are built physically, and how they interact with their environments.

so she decided to go to the University of Michigan Medical School. While she was there, she discovered her passion for helping people with medical problems. She specialized in pediatric neurosurgery, which meant she performed operations on children who had brain diseases or injuries.

Her advisers discouraged her from a career in pediatric neurosurgery and she had trouble finding an internship, but she didn't give up! Finally, she was accepted as an intern at **Yale New Haven Hospital** in 1975, where she was the first woman to join the program. After that, Alexa worked for many years as a pediatric neurosurgeon at Detroit's **Henry Ford** Hospital. She retired and moved to Florida in 2001, but she didn't stay retired for very long! After discovering there were no pediatric neurosurgeons working in her area, she went back to work part-time at Pensacola's Sacred Heart Hospital.

Alexa has been quoted as saying, "The greatest challenge I faced in becoming a neurosurgeon was believing it was possible." Alexa retired for a second time in 2012. She continues to encourage young women to go into medicine and neurosurgery.

A is for Alexa

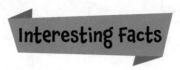

Interesting Facts

Lansing, Michigan
Lansing, Michigan, was also home to Malcom X, the famous minister. His parents bought a home in the Westmont subdivision of the city and in 1929, they were sued because the city had laws in place that said Black families could not live there. There is a historical marker in Lansing that marks the site of Malcolm X's childhood home.

Yale New Haven Hospital
During the Civil War, more than 25,000 US Army officers fighting for the Union were admitted to Yale New Haven Hospital, which temporarily changed its name during the war to the Knight US General Army Hospital.

Henry Ford
Henry Ford's Ford Motor Company was once the leading employer of Blacks in the automotive industry. In 1923, he employed 2,500 Black employees. The wages Ford paid his Black employees were equal to those his white workers earned, and many of his Black employees were skilled laborers.

Benjamin Banneker

"The color of the skin is in no way connected with strength of the mind or intellectual powers."

Benjamin Banneker was an **astronomer**, which means he studied the positions and movements of the sun, moon, and stars through the sky. He was also a farmer, a **surveyor** (someone who studies maps and land boundaries), and a writer. He was born in 1731 in **Baltimore County, Maryland**. His mother was a freed **indentured servant** (a person who agrees to work for a certain number of years for food and shelter), and his father was a freed slave from **Guinea in Africa**. Because both of his parents were free, Benjamin was also born free. Not much is known about his early life, but Benjamin did learn reading, writing, and **arithmetic**, too. He

Words You Should Know

» **Astronomer**: An astronomer is a scientist who studies the movement of stars, planets, and other objects in the sky.

» **Surveyor**: A surveyor measures land and marks boundaries of property.

» **Arithmetic**: Arithmetic is the study of mathematics and numbers.

may have spent some time in a **Quaker** school near his farm. Quakers were a group of people who were against slavery and believed in the equality of all people.

When he was twenty-one, Benjamin built a wooden clock that kept accurate time and rang a bell every hour. The clock ran for more than fifty years. He also built an irrigation system for his farm that helped the crops get water. He taught himself about the movements of the sun, moon, and stars and accurately predicted eclipses of the sun and moon. He was so smart that he caught the attention of the Ellicotts, a wealthy family who lived nearby. They lent him books from their library, which Benjamin used to study astronomy and other subjects that interested him.

In 1791, Andrew Ellicott hired Benjamin to assist him with surveying the nation's capital city, **Washington, DC.** But Benjamin is most famous for a series of **almanacs** he published between 1792 and 1797. Almanacs were short books that told people when there were going to be eclipses and high tides. They also had short articles and opinion columns in them. Benjamin's predictions of high tides were especially helpful to fisherman who needed to know when to fish. Benjamin also figured out the life cycle of the seventeen-year **locust**, an insect that hatches every seventeen years. He was known for conducting scientific experiments on his farm. Late in life, Benjamin wrote a series of letters to President **Thomas Jefferson**, urging him to end slavery and make sure that all people were treated equally. **He died in 1806,** just a month before his seventy-fifth birthday.

B is for Benjamin

Interesting Facts

Baltimore County, Maryland

The first slaves came to Baltimore County, Maryland, during the 1600s, where they were sold at auctions. Baltimore County later became an important stop on the Underground Railroad because it was close to Pennsylvania, where slavery was outlawed. Slaves who were escaping would pass through on their way north. Both Frederick Douglass, a famous abolitionist, and Harriet Tubman, a conductor on the Underground Railroad, came from Maryland.

Indentured servant

Indentured servants were people who agreed to work for a certain number of years, usually between four and seven, in exchange for passage to the New World and a small plot of land. The first indentured servants that came to North America in the early 1600s were mostly white, and because there were no slave laws when Black Africans first came to North America in the 1600s, the first Blacks to arrive were treated as indentured servants, too. Just like white indentured servants, Black indentured servants were given their freedom at the end of their contracts. This all changed when slavery became a rule of law in Virginia, and many Black indentured servants lost their hope of freedom.

Guinea, Africa

The West African nation of Guinea played a major role in the Atlantic slave trade. Europeans arrived in Guinea in the 1600s, kidnapped people from Guinea and other African nations, and traded them as slaves in North America and the Caribbean. Guinea was a French colony until 1958, when they won their freedom from France.

Quaker

Quakers believe that all people are created equal, and that slavery is wrong. The Quakers began openly opposing slavery in the 1600s, almost as soon as the first African slaves arrived in North America. In 1776, they were forbidden from owning slaves by their church, and fourteen years later, they petitioned Congress to end slavery. Many Quakers were active in the abolitionist movement and helped slaves escape through the Underground Railroad.

Washington, DC

Washington, DC, is the capital city of the United States. It was founded in 1790 and is named after George Washington, the first US president and a founder of the country. The White House, Congress, and the Supreme Court are all located in Washington, DC, along with the Smithsonian Institution, a museum dedicated to science and nature.

Almanacs

Some of the oldest almanacs date back to ancient Egypt, where lists of good and bad moments of each day were written. They were used to predict the flooding of the Nile River and different star movements.

Locusts

Locusts (also called cicadas) are a group of insects that live underground for most of their lives. They come out of the ground in different cycles to breed. Benjamin studied the seventeen-year locust, which goes underground for an amazing seventeen years before it comes out to breed.

Thomas Jefferson

Thomas Jefferson was the third US president. He wrote the Declaration of Independence, which sparked the American Revolution. Despite writing in the Declaration of Independence that "all men are created equal," Jefferson was a slave owner, and kept many slaves on his farm at Monticello in Virginia.

Benjamin's death and funeral

During Benjamin's funeral, his farmhouse caught on fire and most of his writings and personal possessions, including the clock he built, were destroyed.

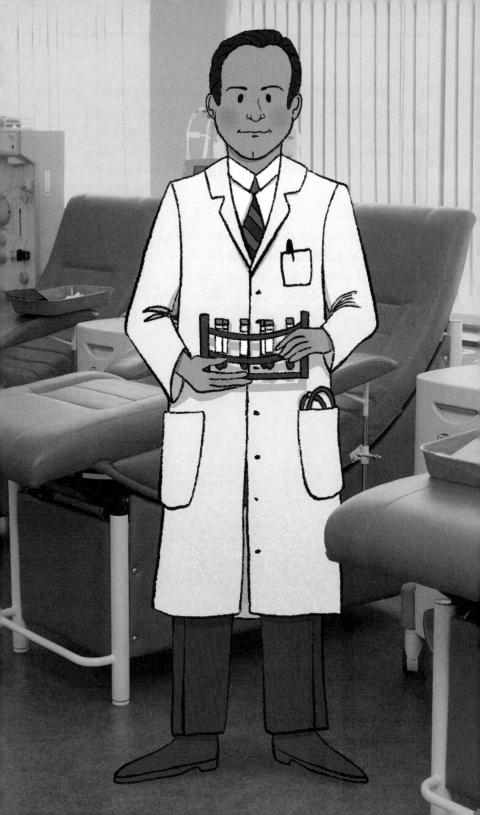

Charles Drew

"The blood of individual human beings may differ from blood groupings, but there is absolutely no scientific basis to indicate any difference in human blood from race to race."

Dr. **Charles Drew** was a surgeon and medical researcher. His work helped develop storage methods for blood and changed the way we do **blood transfusions**. He helped establish the world's first blood bank and invented the **bloodmobile**, an easier method of collecting blood from donations that stored it in a refrigerated truck. He was born in 1904 in Washington, DC, and lived with his family in a middle-class neighborhood in the nation's capital. He earned an athletic scholarship to **Amherst College** in 1922, where he was one of only thirteen Black Americans out of six hundred students.

Charles was a gifted athlete and won the **Mossman Award** for contributing the most to sports during his time at Amherst, but he didn't have an easy time while he was at school there! He faced a lot of discrimination as one of the few Black athletes. His team passed him over for the position of captain even though he was the best athlete on the team, and he often faced prejudice from the teams Amherst played against, but he never gave up!

Words You Should Know

» **Segregation**: Segregation is the separation of people by race.

» **Neuroanatomy**: Neuroanatomy is the study of how the nervous system, including the brain and nerves, is structured.

Charles did not have much of an interest in anything besides sports until one of his biology professors helped him find a passion for medicine. He attended medical school at McGill University in **Montreal, Canada**. At the time, the medical field was very **segregated**, and there were few opportunities for Black Americans in the medical profession. While in medical school, Charles won a scholarship competition in **neuroanatomy** and graduated second in his class of 137 students. He wanted to study further at the Mayo Clinic, but racial prejudice kept many Black doctors from studying where they wanted to go, and so he went to **Howard University**, a traditionally Black college instead. While there, he became a professor and was the chief medical resident at Freedmen's Hospital.

When he finished his internship at Howard University, Charles went to Columbia University to earn his doctorate in medicine. He was awarded a scholarship that would have given him direct access to patients, but because of racial prejudice, he was assigned to work with John Scudder who was working on starting a blood bank, which would allow donated blood to be stored for longer periods of time. Although he did not work directly with patients, Charles ended up saving thousands of lives! His research with John Scudder led to a position with the Blood for Britain Project, a program that collected blood from American citizens to be sent to Great Britain to help soldiers and civilians. It was very early in **World War II**, and Great Britain was under attack by Germany. Charles's work with the Blood for Britain Project prevented thousands of people wounded in the war from dying.

After he finished with the Blood for Britain Project, he went on to work for the American Red Cross. He set up their blood banks and invented the bloodmobile, but the America Red Cross had rules that prevented Blacks from donating their blood, even though there is no difference in blood between races. This meant that Charles couldn't donate blood to the same program he was running! He spoke out against the rules, and the Red Cross eventually allowed Black people to donate their blood, but donations remained segregated until 1950, so a white person and a Black person couldn't donate blood to each other.

In October 1942, Charles returned to Howard Medical University where he trained Black surgeons and fought against discrimination in the medical field.

C is for Charles

Interesting Facts

Blood transfusion

Although there is no difference in blood between races other than the standard blood types, blood donations were separated by race for a long time. During World War II, Black blood was marked "N" for negro and only given to Black soldiers. Some blood banks refused to accept any Black blood at all! The American Red Cross ended the practice of separating Black blood from other donations in 1950, but Louisiana continued to keep its blood separated by race until 1972.

Bloodmobile

The bloodmobile is a truck that allows people to donate their blood anywhere the truck is parked. When the bloodmobile was first invented, the American Red Cross kept Black blood segregated from white blood. The bloodmobile's creator Dr. Charles Drew wasn't allowed to donate his own blood to white patients in need of transfusions because he was Black. This all changed in 1950, the year Charles died. Bloodmobiles are still being used today, so that people who need blood can get it more easily.

Amherst College

Edward Jones was the first Black student to graduate from Amherst College in 1826, which was a time when most Black people did not attend college at all!

Mossman Award

Amherst College's Mossman Award is given to the graduating senior who brings the most honor to their team in athletics in both achievement and sportsmanship.

Montreal, Canada

Black Canadians make up about 10.3 percent of Montreal's population and are roughly 171,000 in number. Most Black Canadians are of African or Caribbean descent, and there are many Black African American descendants in Montreal.

Howard University

Howard University, a traditionally Black college, opened in 1867, in Washington, DC. It is named for General Oliver Otis Howard, who worked for the Freedmen's Bureau after the Civil War to help former slaves adjust to freedom. The school has always allowed students of any color to attend, but is known for its rich history of Black students. Among some of the notable people who have attended Howard University are playwright Amiri Baraka and writer Toni Morrison.

World War II

During World War II, 1.2 million Black soldiers served in the military. They were subject to segregation and treated poorly because of their race. Most Black soldiers during the war served behind the scenes because they were considered unfit for combat or leadership roles. But at the end of the war, when they were really needed, Black soldiers began to serve in limited front-line roles. The Tuskegee Airman, a group of Black soldiers from Tuskegee, Alabama, flew 1,600 missions over Italy, destroying 237 German aircrafts on the ground and 37 in the air.

Daniel Hale Williams

"A people who don't make provisions for their own sick and suffering are not worthy of civilization."

Dr. **Daniel Hale Williams** was a surgeon who founded the first Black-owned hospital, and the first Black **cardiologist** to perform successful open-heart surgery. He was born in 1856 in Hollidaysburg, **Pennsylvania**. His father died of **tuberculosis** when he was nine years old. His mother, who could not support all of her children on her own, sent Daniel to serve as apprentice to a shoemaker. But Daniel did not like the work and ran away from the shoemaker to rejoin his mother. He later opened a barber shop, but that wasn't the right career for him either.

He became fascinated with the medical profession and apprenticed under a doctor for two years before going to study medicine at Chicago Medical School, where he earned his degree in 1883. After he graduated from medical school, Daniel opened his own practice where he saw both Black and white patients. Most private hospitals at the time

Words You Should Know

» **Cardiologist**: A cardiologist is a doctor who specializes in heart disease and abnormalities.

» **Tuberculosis**: Tuberculosis is a disease that can attack any part of the body, but usually attacks the lungs. There is a long history of tuberculosis infections, and it continues to be a health problem for many people. Black people are eight times more likely to contract tuberculosis than white people.

did not admit Black patients or hire Black staff, so he opened his own hospital! Provident Hospital in **Chicago, Illinois**, saw both Black and white patients and had an integrated staff, which was amazing and exciting for the time. He also set up a program at Provident to train Black doctors and nurses.

In 1893, Daniel became the first Black cardiologist to perform successful open-heart surgery when he operated on a man who had been stabbed in the heart. Daniel performed the surgery without many of the tools doctors now use, and after the surgery, his patient lived for another twenty years! He wasn't allowed to join the **American Medical Association** because he was Black, so he started his own organization for Black doctors: **The National Medical Association**. He was the first Black doctor admitted to the **American College of Surgeons**. Daniel also opened and ran two training programs for Black nurses during his career. He died in 1931.

D is for Daniel

Interesting Facts

Pennsylvania

Pennsylvania, one of the southernmost free states during slavery, was a major destination for slaves escaping to freedom on the Underground Railroad. Once they crossed the border into Pennsylvania, slaves were considered free.

Chicago, Illinois

Chicago is the biggest city in Illinois. It has a population of more than two million people. After the Civil War, when many slaves moved north, they went to Chicago to start new lives. Chicago has a rich culture and is known for its jazz music. The city of Chicago was first settled in the 1780s by a Black and French explorer from Haiti named Jean Baptiste Point du Sable.

American Medical Association

The American Medical Association is the largest organization of doctors in the United States. It was founded in 1847. The American Medical Association issued an apology to the National Medical Association in 2008 for more than a hundred years of excluding Black physicians from their group and for preventing them from joining other medical societies.

The National Medical Association

The National Medical Association was founded in 1895. It is still active today, and serves the interests of doctors of African descent and their patients. During the time of Jim Crow, Black physicians were separated from white physicians by laws that kept them out of white medical societies, including the American Medical Association. Twelve Black doctors formed the National Medical Association to give Black doctors a voice on important issues relating to medicine. Today, the National Medical Association has more than 30,000 members.

American College of Surgeons

The American College of Surgeons is an educational society for surgeons that was founded in 1912. In order to become part of the American College of Surgeons, a doctor must pass a difficult series of tests to prove their skills at surgery. The American College of Surgeons has over 82,000 members.

Elijah McCoy

Elijah McCoy was an amazing inventor who was born in 1844 in Colchester, Ontario, **Canada**. His parents were runaway slaves who had escaped with their eleven children from Kentucky to Canada on the **Underground Railroad!** Elijah's parents could tell he was incredibly smart, so they sent him all the way to Edinburgh, **Scotland**, to study engineering and apprentice under a mechanical engineer. When he finished school, his parents moved back to the United States to a town called **Ypsilanti**, in Michigan, where his father made cigars on a farm.

Even with his education, Elijah could only find work as a fireman and oiler on the railroad, but he put his mind to the job and invented an automatic **lubricator** to keep **steam engines** from overheating. He applied for his first **patent** (an official registration of an invention) in 1872. His invention became known as "the real McCoy"— people found it so effective that they asked for it by name!

Words You Should Know

» **Lubricator**: A lubricator is a mechanism that injects oil into an engine to make it run more smoothly and reduce friction. This helps keep the engine from getting too hot.

» **Patent**: A patent is a license that allows a person or company to be the only one to manufacture an invention for use.

During his career, he applied for fifty-seven patents, including the automatic lawn sprinkler and a folding ironing board. However, he is best known for his automatic steam engine lubricator, which allowed trains to run farther without having to stop for maintenance. Elijah died in 1929 in Detroit, Michigan.

E is for Elijah

When a person wanted one of Elijah McCoy's lubricators, they would ask for "the real McCoy." This phrase became famous and people would use it to talk about anything that was genuine.

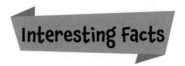

Interesting Facts

Canada

Slavery was legal in some parts of Canada until 1834. Once it became illegal to own slaves in Canada, American slaves began running for the Canadian border and escaping to freedom.

Underground Railroad

The Underground Railroad was a network of safe houses and secret routes that slaves used to escape to free states and Canada during slavery. Slaves were helped on their journeys by abolitionists and other people who thought slavery was wrong and should end. People started using the Underground Railroad in the 1700s, and it continued to be used until slavery ended. Some estimates say that up to 100,000 slaves escaped to freedom on the Underground Railroad. During its busiest years, up to 1,000 slaves a year were escaping to freedom by using the path north. Harriet Tubman, who was an escaped slave herself, was one of the most famous conductors on the Underground Railroad.

Scotland

Slavery was legal in Scotland until 1778, and many wealthy people considered it fashionable to own slaves to work in their homes. Many Scottish landowners were also active in sugar plantations in the Caribbean and owned slaves on Caribbean islands that were colonies of the British Empire.

Ypsilanti, Michigan

Ypsilanti is a small city in Michigan. It was first settled in 1823. Its name comes from a Greek war hero, Demetrios Ypsilantis, who fought in the Greek War for Independence. Ypsilanti has a 29 percent Black population and was once important to the automobile industry. Ford Motor Company had a manufacturing plant in Ypsilanti where they made B-24 bombers for World War II. ACE, Tucker, Kaiser, and Frazer automobiles were also once made there.

Steam engines

A steam engine uses the pressure of heated steam to move a piston in a circular motion. The first trains were run by steam engines. A train would heat the steam in its engine by using a coal fire to warm water past its boiling point, transforming the water into steam and expanding it in size. Steam engines are prone to accidental explosions when they overheat, and are only used in trains in China today.

Flemmie Pansy Kittrell

Dr. **Flemmie Pansy Kittrell** was born in 1904 in Henderson, **North Carolina**. She was the first Black woman to earn a **PhD** (which stands for Doctor of Philosophy) in **nutrition**, and the first Black woman to receive her PhD from **Cornell University**. She was the seventh of nine children born to James and Alice Kittrell, and her family background was mixed **Cherokee** and African American. Flemmie's parents made sure that education was very important in their home. Flemmie's father read **short stories and poems** to the family. She graduated high school with honors and her family encouraged her to go to Hampton Institute for a degree in **home economics**. Her professors were so impressed with her work at Hampton that they encouraged her to go to graduate school.

Very few Black women—very few women of any race—attended graduate school at the time, but Flemmie won a scholarship to Cornell University, a prestigious **Ivy League college**. Flemmie graduated from Cornell with a master's degree in 1930, and received a PhD from Cornell in 1936. In the early years of her career she taught high school, but she soon accepted a position at

Words You Should Know

» **PhD**: PhD is short for Doctor of Philosophy. It is an advanced college degree that allows people who earn it to teach their subject in universities or to get a job in their specialized field of work.

» **Nutrition**: Nutrition is the study of how to get the right foods for growth and health.

» **Home economics**: Home economics is the study of cooking and housework.

Bennett College in Greensboro, North Carolina. She later returned to Hampton Institute as a professor of nutrition and quickly became the dean of the school of home economics.

In 1947, Flemmie began an international crusade to help children suffering from hunger She believed that the lack of access to food was a huge problem for poor people, and so she combined her home economic classes with courses in science and engineering to try to solve it. She traveled to **Liberia** in Africa where she discovered that, while Liberian people typically had full bellies, they weren't receiving enough nutrients on their diets of cassava and rice. She introduced different ways to add more protein into their diets, such as through fishing. Flemmie traveled the world in pursuit of her studies. Along with Liberia, she traveled to **India**, Japan, West Africa, Central Africa, Guinea, and Russia. She helped set up a training program for home economics in Baroda College in India. And back at Howard, Flemmie used her position to recruit students from all over the world. In the 1960s, she helped establish the Head Start program for pre-kindergarten children. She was awarded the Scroll of Honor from the **National Council of Negro Women** in 1961. She died in 1980.

F is for Flemmie

Interesting Facts

North Carolina

Slavery was legal in North Carolina from colonial times up until the Emancipation Proclamation. North Carolina was the last state to join the Confederacy. Even after slavery ended, discrimination was still a big problem in North Carolina because of Jim Crow laws that kept Black people separate from white people.

Cornell University

Cornell University is an Ivy League college in Ithaca, New York. It was founded in 1865. There are no statistics on how many Black students attended Cornell in the late 1800s, but in 1886, it was the only major institution in the United States to admit both male and female Black students.

Cherokee

The Cherokee lived in the Southeast United States for many years. They had their own alphabet and written language; they also owned Cherokee indigenous slaves, even before white people settled in their region. After their region was colonized by white settlers, the Cherokee began to purchase African slaves to work on their plantations and in their homes. They were forced off their land by the Indian Removal Act in the 1830s and relocated to reservations in the western US. They took their slaves with them on the long march west, and bought more once they resettled on reservations. Today, the Cherokee live mainly in North Carolina and Oklahoma.

Short stories and poems in Black communities

It was illegal for slaves to learn to read and write, so most stories and poems were passed down orally from generation to generation for many years. Stories and poems are important to many Black people, going back to their origins in Africa, where stories were also passed down. Once they were allowed to read and write, free Black people began to write down their stories and poems. Groups of Black writers would sometimes get together to share their stories and poems, which led to movements in art and culture. One example is the Harlem Renaissance in New York that led to the rise in popularity of Black writers like Zora Neale Hurston, Langston Hughes, and others. During the civil rights movement, another wave of popular Black writers rose to the forefront with writers like Maya Angelou, Ralph Ellison, Amiri Baraka, and Lorraine Hansberry. Today, there are many Black storytellers and poets, and poetry and stories continue to be an important part of Black culture.

Ivy League college

The Ivy League colleges are Brown University, Columbia University, Cornell University, Dartmouth College, Harvard University, the University of Pennsylvania, Princeton University, and Yale University. The name "Ivy League" was at first used to describe a sports conference between the schools, but has come to mean that these are elite, prestigious colleges. They are very difficult to get into, and students must work hard to earn good grades at these schools. Historically, they have had low numbers of Black students. They continue to enroll low numbers of Black students compared to other races.

Liberia

Liberia is a country on the west coast of Africa. It started as a settlement for Black people in the United States and the Caribbean by the African Colonization Society, who believed that Black people would have a better chance at freedom if they were moved from the United States and the Caribbean and sent back to live in Africa, where they and their ancestors were born. Liberia was the first African nation to declare its independence, which it did in 1847. It continues to be an independent nation today.

India

India is a country in South Asia. It has the second highest population in the world. India has a very long history—people have been living there for 55,000 years since they first moved there from Africa! India was an important country on the spice trading routes because they grew many spices there that European and Middle Eastern traders wanted to buy and sell. For a long time, India was a colony of Great Britain and used slave labor to work on their plantations and in wealthy people's homes. It gained its independence from Great Britain in 1947.

National Council of Negro Women

The National Council of Negro Women (NCNW) was founded in 1896 as the National Council of Colored Women. It was the first national, Black-run organization in the United States. Its members were middle-class, educated Black women who wanted to join together to make their communities safer, more unified, and better educated. The NCNW has fought against racism, lynchings, and they have helped women join the military.

Garrett Augustus Morgan

"If you can be the best, then why not try to be the best?"

Garrett Augustus Morgan Sr. was a Black inventor, **community leader**, and businessman. He was born in 1877 in Claysville, Harrison County, **Kentucky**. His father was the son of a freed slave of **Confederate** General John H. Morgan, of **Morgan's Raiders**. His mother was a slave who was part Native American. He had at least one brother. With a sixth-grade education from Claysville's Branch Elementary School, Garrett moved at the age of fourteen to Cincinnati, Ohio, in search of work. Like many American children at the time, Garrett had to quit school to work full time to help support his family, but he was able to hire a tutor to help him continue his studies.

In Cincinnati, he found work repairing **sewing machines**. The mechanics of his new job sparked his creativity and inventiveness, and he discovered many ways to improve the machines he worked with. He began trying out his ideas and built his first invention while working there. It was a belt fastener for sewing machines. In 1907, he opened his own sewing machine shop, and helped start the **Cleveland Association of Colored Men**.

His inventive mind didn't only focus on sewing machines, though! Garrett also invented a safety hood for firefighters with eye goggles that allowed them to see through a smoky room, with tubes that ran beneath the smoke so they could breathe in oxygen. He even successfully rescued two men who were trapped in an explosion underneath **Lake Erie**. But in order to sell his product in the South, he had to hire a white man to pretend to be the inventor, while he entered smoke-filled areas to demonstrate his product. His fire hood invention became the model for gas masks used during World War II.

Garrett also invented the modern **three-light traffic signal** to warn people when they would have to come to a stop. In 1913, he invented a **hair straightening cream** which he sold along with hair coloring and a straightening comb that he also invented. He died in 1963.

G is for Garrett

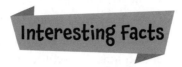

Interesting Facts

Community leaders

Community leaders are important to the Black community because they help Black people get together and organize change. During slavery, it was difficult for slaves to communicate with each other because they didn't have rights. Community leaders help make sure that Black people have rights and can fix problems in the world. Community leaders bring attention to problems in the Black community, and have helped pass laws that ensure Black people have civil rights and are treated more equally.

Kentucky

Kentucky is a southern state in the United States. It was the fifteenth state to enter the Union and was split off from Virginia. Kentucky is known for thoroughbred horse racing and Kentucky bluegrass. It has the largest cave system in the world. Kentucky was part of the Confederacy during the Civil War and was a slave state.

Confederacy

The Confederacy was a group of southern states that split off from the Union over the issue of slavery and declared independence. Their decision to leave the Union led to the Civil War.

Morgan's Raiders

Morgan's Raiders were a group of Confederate soldiers who rode into the states of West Virginia, Indiana, Kentucky, and Ohio during the Civil War. They were trying to distract Union forces from the front lines in Vicksburg and Gettysburg. The raiders are named for Brigadier General John Hunt Morgan who led their forces. The raid covered over a thousand miles and lasted longer than a month. In the end they were not successful, but they did scare people living in the North who had not seen much fighting during the Civil War.

Sewing machines

The first sewing machine was invented by the British inventor Thomas Saint in 1790. It wasn't sold very successfully, but could sew through leather and canvas. Sewing machines became more popular in the 1800s once the design was improved. It revolutionized the clothing industry because people could sew clothes faster with it. Before sewing machines, people had to sew their clothing by hand, and it took a long time!

Cleveland Association of Colored Men

The Cleveland Association of Colored Men was founded in June 1908 by Black businessmen and professionals to help improve the economic and social conditions of Black people. The Cleveland Association of Colored Men brought community leaders together for lectures, social events, charitable projects, and weekly public meetings.

Lake Erie

Lake Erie is the eleventh largest lake in the world and fourth in size out of the five Great Lakes in North America. It is bordered by Canada on the north and Michigan, Pennsylvania, Ohio, and New York in the United States. Lake Erie is fed by the Detroit River, and is used for hydroelectric power.

Traffic signals

The world's first traffic light was gas-powered and needed to be operated by hand. It was placed at an intersection in London in 1868 and exploded less than a month after it was put up, injuring the policeman who was operating it.

Hair straightening

Hair straightening has been happening since ancient Egypt, when two flat iron plates were heated to straighten hair. But this led to many people getting burnt! Hair straightening became popular in the 1890s and later in the 1950s among Black people. People use a combination of heated irons and chemical relaxers to straighten their hair and give it a sleek appearance.

George Washington Carver

"Education is the key to unlock the golden door of freedom."

George Washington Carver was an agricultural scientist and inventor who promoted alternative crops to cotton, and alternative methods to make soil produce more crops. He was known as the most prominent Black scientist of the early twentieth century. Because he was born into slavery in Diamond, Missouri, no one knows exactly when he was born, but it was probably between 1860–1865. When he was just a week old, some raiders kidnapped George, his mother, his brother James, and his sister and sold them in Kentucky! George never saw his mother again.

After slavery was abolished, George returned to the home of Moses Carver, the plantation owner who owned him before he was kidnapped. Moses raised George as his own son, and Moses's wife taught George how to read and write. Because Black children were not allowed to attend the public school near his home, George traveled ten miles to attend the closest Black school he could find. When he was thirteen, he traveled to **Kansas City** to attend a Black academy but left after he witnessed the murder of a Black man by a group of white men. He eventually made his way to **Minneapolis, Minnesota**, where he earned his high school degree. George applied to many colleges before being accepted to Highland University in Highland, Kansas, but when he got there, they refused to let

---

Words You Should Know

» **Raiders**: Raiders are people who attack business places or homes in order to steal.

---

him attend the school because he was Black! In 1883, unable to attend college, George staked a claim on a lot of land where he plowed seventeen acres by hand and planted rice, corn, Indian corn, and other vegetables, as well as fruit trees, forest trees, and shrubbery. He made extra money by doing odd jobs in town and working as a ranch hand.

In 1888, George was given a three-hundred-dollar loan from the Bank of Ness City for his education. In 1890, George started studying piano and art at Simpson College in **Iowa**. One of his professors recognized George's talent for painting flowers and plants and encouraged him to study botany at Iowa State Agricultural College. George was the first Black student at Iowa State, and he continued there for his master's degree, studying plant diseases and fungus. His work during that time earned him national recognition as a **botanist** (someone who studies plants). When he earned his master's degree, he became the first Black faculty member at Iowa State. In 1896, **Booker T. Washington** invited George to go work at the Tuskegee Institute, where his research really took off. In addition to teaching farmers how to rotate crops to keep the soil fertile, he developed over 105 recipes for the peanut, and made similar studies of the sweet potato.

Words You Should Know

» **Botanist**: A botanist is an expert or student who studies plant life.

» **Environmentalism**: Environmentalism is a movement that seeks to reduce the harm that people do to nature through activities like pollution or destroying natural places.

George worked hard to improve the lives of farmers and was an advocate for **environmentalism**. He developed a mobile classroom called a **Jesup Agricultural Wagon** to take from place to place to educate farmers. At a time when few non-Black papers carried news about Black scientists, George was well-known and praised in many communities. He received many honors for his work, including the Spingarn Medal from the **NAACP**. He died on January 5, 1943.

G is also for George

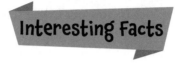

Interesting Facts

Kansas City

Founded in 1850, Kansas City is the largest city in Missouri. It is rich in Black culture and history. Kansas City is known for jazz, barbecue, and as home to a museum dedicated to the Negro Leagues in baseball.

Minneapolis, Minnesota

Minneapolis is the largest city in Minnesota. It was founded in 1867. Minneapolis is known for its many rivers and lakes. It also has a thriving music scene and was home to Prince, as well as hip hop and rap artists Lizzo, Brother Ali, Atmosphere, and Dessa. Minneapolis has had some issues with racism. In 1910, a real estate developer began writing exclusions on his deeds that prevented Black people and Asians from owning or leasing certain properties. Other real estate developers copied this practice, even though it was outlawed in 1953. As recently as 2017, the racist practice of excluding Black people and Asians from leasing some properties was still being written onto deeds in the city. In this same city in 2020, a white policeman was captured on camera kneeling on George Floyd's neck for eight minutes. When George Floyd died because of this, protests erupted all over the world and because of this incident the Black Lives Matter movement gained more traction in raising awareness about police brutality against Black people.

Iowa

Iowa is a midwestern state in the United States. It was first explored by Europeans in the 1600s and was a colony of France, and later Spain, before it became the twenty-ninth state in the United States in 1846. It was a free state during the Civil War. Iowa is known for its corn fields and farms, and has been voted one of the safest states to live in.

Booker T. Washington

Born in 1856, Booker T. Washington was part of the last generation born into slavery, and became one of the leading voices for civil rights during his generation. He was an author, educator, speaker, and adviser to presidents between 1890 and 1915! He founded the Tuskegee Institute in Alabama, a historical Black college. He is known for calling for the advancement of Black people through education and entrepreneurship.

Jesup Wagon

The Jesup Agricultural Wagon was part of the Tuskegee Institute's Movable Education Program and was filled with soil samples, seeds, recipes, farm equipment, and other materials used to teach farmers about farming. It was named for Morris K. Jesup, who gave the money to build the first wagon and equip it with mules to pull it.

NAACP

The National Association for the Advancement of Colored People is the oldest and largest civil rights organization in the United States. It was formed in 1909 by a group of Black and white activists who wanted conditions for Black people to improve. The NAACP has been active in passing civil rights laws and in organizing protests like the 1963 March on Washington. Today, it has more than 500,000 members!

Henry Brown

Henry Brown was an inventor best known for creating a fireproof safe for storing documents. Very little is known about Henry other than that he was a Black inventor. He designed a desktop document storage box that was fireproof and could be locked. At the time, most people kept their private documents either at home or stored in a safe deposit box at the bank. But there was no way to ensure privacy at the bank, and a burglar could easily break into someone's home and steal their valuable documents. What little we know about Henry is on his 1886 patent application for the **strongbox**. We know he lived in Washington, DC, and that very few Black inventors were applying for patents when he patented his strongbox. His strongbox later became the prototype for the modern day safe, which is still widely used in offices and homes today!

Words You Should Know

» **Strongbox**: A strongbox is a small box that can be locked. It's usually made of metal and is used for storing valuables.

Isaac R. Johnson

Isaac **R. Johnson** was an American inventor famous for inventing the **folding bicycle frame**. Much of Isaac's life is a mystery. We do know that he was born in **New York** sometime in 1812. While it was very difficult for Black Americans to file successful patents during the late 1800s, Isaac's patent was approved. You'd recognize the shape of the bicycle frame he designed. It's very similar to the bicycle frames of today, but his was also designed to fold up into small pieces to be stored away, which came in handy for traveling.

Several Black inventors worked on the bicycle besides Isaac, including Matthew Cherry and Jerry Certain. Matthew Cherry made improvements to the first type of bicycle (which did not have pedals), and patented the tricycle (which many people still use today). Jerry Certain invented "parcel carriers," which would attach to bicycles and allow the rider to carry packages on the bike frame.

Bicycles are an important part of Black History. After the Civil War, the US army formed all-Black infantries also known as "**buffalo soldiers**." The buffalo soldiers traveled 1,900 miles by bicycle from Montana to Missouri to test the use of bicycles in the military and see if a bicycle was good for transporting troops!

I is for Issac

Interesting Facts

Folding bicycle

The first folding bicycles were developed in the 1890s in France for use by the army. During World War II, the British Army developed a folding bike that weighed just thirty-two pounds and could be dropped by parachute to the troops below. It was designed to land on its handlebars and seat, since landing on its wheels might damage it.

New York City

New York City is the largest city in the United States, and the largest city in the world by landmass. It is home to over eight million people, so it's also one of the biggest cities in the world due to the size of its population! New York was first settled in 1624 by Dutch colonists. New York was the capital of the United States from 1785 until 1790. As many as eight hundred languages are spoken in New York City. Many of the people who immigrate to the United States come through New York City, and the Statue of Liberty is in New York Harbor as a symbol of greetings to them.

Buffalo Soldiers

Buffalo Soldiers were all-Black cavalry soldiers who served on the western frontier following the Civil War. They were given the nickname "buffalo soldiers" by the Native Americans they encountered. The buffalo soldiers had several jobs, including protecting stagecoaches, settlers, wagon trains, and railroad crews, controlling the Native American population, and catching cattle thieves.

James Edward Maceo West

"In those days in the South, the only professional jobs that seemed to be open to a Black man were a teacher, a preacher, a doctor or a lawyer. My father introduced me to three Black men who had earned doctorates in chemistry and physics. The best jobs they could find were at the post office."

James Edward Maceo West is an American inventor. He helped invent the modern **microphone** and holds over 250 patents! James was born in 1931 in Prince Edward County, Virginia. When he was still young, he had a fascination with how things worked and would take appliances apart. He said, "If I had a screwdriver and a pair of pliers, anything that could be opened was in danger. I had this need to know what was inside."

He knew from a young age that he wanted to be a scientist, but his parents worried he would have trouble finding a job because there were so few Black scientists at the time, and the South was still segregated by **Jim Crow** laws. They pressured him to become a doctor, but he didn't listen. He went to **Temple University** in 1953 to study physics and worked

Words You Should Know

» **Microphone**: A microphone is a device that captures sound waves and converts them to an electronic signal that can either be made louder or converted to digital sound with a recording device.

» **Jim Crow**: Jim Crow laws were a series of laws that Southern states passed to legally separate Black people from white people.

summers as an intern at **Bell Laboratories**. When he graduated from Temple in 1957, he was hired full time at Bell.

In 1960, he and another scientist, Gerhard Sessler, developed the modern microphone. Today, 90 percent of all microphones used are the kind that James and Gerhard created. He was inducted into the National Inventors Hall of Fame in 1999. James has also worked to encourage women and people of color to study science and technology. After he retired from Bell Labs in 2001, he became a professor at **Johns Hopkins University**.

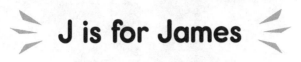

J is for James

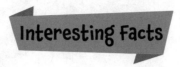

Interesting Facts

Temple University

Temple University is home to the Blockson Afro-American Collection, an exhibit of more than 700,000 pieces of Black American history spanning from 1581 to the present day.

Bell Laboratories

Bell Laboratories is the most successful invention laboratory the world has ever seen. It was founded in 1925, and grew out of several laboratories that Alexander Graham Bell set up after he invented the telephone. It still exists as Nokia Bell Labs, but it's much smaller than it used to be.

Johns Hopkins University

Johns Hopkins University is a private research college in Baltimore, Maryland. It was founded in 1876. Because Maryland was a Southern state where Jim Crow laws were enforced, Johns Hopkins did not admit Black students for most of its history. Kelly Miller was the first Black undergraduate to attend Johns Hopkins from 1887–1889, but most Black students were kept out of Johns Hopkins until the 1950s and 1960s. The school is named after a Quaker abolitionist, Johns Hopkins, who gave seven million dollars to fund the school and a hospital.

Katherine Johnson

"I like to learn. That's an art and a science."

Katherine Johnson was a mathematician whose calculations helped the first US-piloted space flights and many others that followed. She was born in 1918 in White Sulphur Springs, **West Virginia**, and was interested in math from a very young age. Because schools in her hometown did not offer public education to Black students past the eighth grade, Katherine had to travel to attend high school in Institute, West Virginia, on the campus of West Virginia State College. She was so advanced that she began attending high school at the age of ten and graduated at just fourteen years old. She then began college at West Virginia State and very quickly took every math class the college offered. The school added math classes just to accommodate her love of the subject. She graduated with a degree in mathematics and **French** at the age of eighteen.

Katherine wanted to become a research mathematician, but it was difficult to find a career in that field for Black people, especially women. After one of her family members told her that the **National Advisory Committee for Aeronautics** was looking for mathematicians, Katherine applied and was hired.

Words You Should Know

» **NACA**: The National Advisory Committee for Aeronautics was the research institution that later became NASA. It was established in 1915.

Katherine worked as a **human computer**, figuring out things like **gust alleviation** for aircrafts. Her office was segregated, which meant that she had to eat lunch in a different room than her white coworkers and use a separate bathroom, even though she was smarter than many of them! When she first worked for NACA, no women were allowed to put their names on any of the scientific papers they wrote, so her male coworkers often took credit for work she had done.

Words You Should Know

» **Gust alleviation:** Gust alleviation systems are the parts of aircrafts that help them avoid being blown off course by the wind.

» **Aerospace technologist:** Aerospace technologists build, service, test, and repair space crafts. They also keep them running smoothly.

From 1958 until she retired, Katherine worked as an **aerospace technologist**. As part of her job, she calculated the trajectory for the flight of astronaut Alan Shepard, the first American in space. She also calculated the launch window for the 1961 Mercury mission and created navigation charts for astronauts. President Barack Obama presented her with the Presidential Medal of Freedom in 2015. She spent her later years encouraging students to go into science, technology, engineering, or mathematics. Katherine died in 2020.

Katherine Johnson, Dorothy Vaughan, and Mary Jackson were the three women known as the "Hidden Figures." They were a group of Black female mathematicians who worked for NASA and helped launch the space program. There is a 2016 film called *Hidden Figures* that you can watch if you want to learn more about them. It stars Taraji P. Henson, Janelle Monáe, and Octavia Spencer, among others.

K is for Katherine

Interesting Facts

West Virginia

West Virginia is a mid-Atlantic state in the United States. It was the thirty-fifth state to join the Union in 1865, during the Civil War. Some people in West Virginia owned slaves, but most did not. West Virginia is known for coal mining and logging.

Francophone Black nations

Twenty-one nations in Africa have French as their official language, and twenty-nine countries in the world speak French. Some Black nations speak French because they were once colonies of France. Some Black countries that speak French include: Haiti, Congo, Morocco, Madagascar, Cameroon, Ivory Coast, Niger, Burkina Faso, Mali, Senegal, Chad, Tunisia, Guinea, Rwanda, Burundi, Benin, Togo, Central African Republic, Congo, Gabon, Equatorial Guinea, Comoros, and Seychelles.

Human computers

The human computers were a group of women who worked at NACA and made mathematical calculations by hand before modern computers were invented. They were needed to determine lots of different things, like how many rockets were needed to make a plane airborne and what kind of rocket fuel to use. Several Black mathematicians were human computers, but they were segregated from their white coworkers and worked in a separate office. Eventually, computers made it much easier to do the kind of calculations the human computers did by hand.

Lewis Howard Latimer

"Some blessings have been ours in the past, and these may be repeated or even multiplied."

Lewis Howard Latimer was an American inventor and patent draftsman. He helped invent the incandescent lightbulb, among other things. Lewis was born in 1848 in Chelsea, **Massachusetts**. His parents escaped slavery in **Virginia** and fled to Massachusetts, which was a free state. His father had to go to court to win his freedom after he was recognized and arrested just a few days after arriving in Boston.

When Lewis was young, he worked with his father in a barbershop and at night, they worked hanging wallpaper. When he was ten years old, his father fled in fear of being enslaved again, and Lewis's mother, who could not afford to support her four children, sent Lewis and his brothers to a farm school. When he was fifteen years old, Lewis joined the **US Navy** and worked on the USS Massasoit, a steamer ship. After he left the Navy, Lewis found work as an office boy with a patent law firm, where he drew sketches for patents after he taught himself technical drawing.

Alexander Graham Bell hired Lewis to draw the sketches for his patent for the telephone. Lewis received a patent for a carbon filament for incandescent lightbulbs and invented an early version of the **air conditioner**. He co-patented an improved toilet for railroad cars. He also wrote a **book of poetry**, played the violin and flute, painted portraits, and wrote plays. He died in 1928.

L is for Lewis

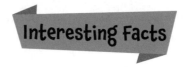

Interesting Facts

Massachusetts

Massachusetts is a state in the New England region of the United States. It was first settled in 1620 at Plymouth by colonists from England. It was the sixth state to enter the Union. Massachusetts was a free state during the Civil War. Many of the abolitionists who tried to end slavery came from Massachusetts. Boston is its capital and largest city, and was the site of the gunshot that started the Revolutionary War.

Virginia

Virginia is a mid-Atlantic state in the United States and was the tenth state to join the Union in 1788. The first colony in the New World was started in Virginia in 1607! During the Civil War, the vote to join the Confederacy was split in Virginia, and West Virginia split off from Virginia in order to become a free state. Virginia had many slave plantations and relied heavily on slave labor before the Civil War.

Blacks in the US Navy

Black sailors have been serving in the US Navy since it first started in 1781. Throughout much of its history, the Navy was segregated, and Black sailors served separately from their white counterparts. But Black sailors have fought in every war the US has been in. There are fifteen naval ships named for Black Americans: USS Doris Miller, USS Oscar Austin, USNS Carl Brashear, USS Jesse L. Brown, USS George Washington Carver,

USNS Charlton, USS Rodney M. Davis, USNS Charles Drew, USNS Medgar Evers, USS Gravely, USS Harmon, USNS Henson, USS Miller, USS Pinckney, and the USNS Watson.

Alexander Graham Bell

The inventor Alexander Graham Bell was born in Scotland in 1847. Both his mother and wife were deaf, so he experimented with hearing devices to try to help deaf people hear. This led to his invention of the telephone. He also worked in telecommunications and aerospace technology. He died in 1922.

Air conditioner

People have been trying to cool down since ancient Egypt! In Egypt, they used water to cool the air by dripping it outside a room and surrounding the room with humid air. This was helpful in the desert, where the air is very dry. Benjamin Franklin and John Hadley performed the first mechanical air conditioning experiment in 1758. They were able to cool a thermometer past the freezing point by evaporating liquids to cool off the air surrounding the thermometer. The first electric air conditioner was developed in 1902.

Lewis's poetry and plays

In addition to his inventions, Lewis Latimer painted portraits, played the flute and violin, and wrote poetry and plays. He had a book of poems published called *Poems of Love and Life*.

Friends

Friend of my childhood,
Of life's early days
When together we wandered
Through bright sunny ways
Each true to the other,
Till full manhood came,
And found the old friendship
As ever the same.

Came summer and winter,
Years waxed and waned.
Youth it had left us
But friendship remained
And now as with white locks
I bend o'er life's page,
The friend of my childhood
Is the friend of my age.

Marie Van Brittan Brown

Marie Van Brittan Brown was an American inventor. She
and her husband, Albert Brown, invented the **home
security system**. Marie was born in **Queens, New York**, in 1922.
She worked as a nurse, and her husband was an electrician
who was often away nights. Police in her neighborhood were
slow to respond to **emergency calls** and the crime rate in her
neighborhood was high. She wanted a way to see who was at
her front door from any room in her house, so she invented a
home security system!

The system had four peepholes so people of different
heights could be seen through the door, where she also had a
camera pointed toward the peepholes. She set up television
monitors and two-way microphones so she could both see
and speak to the person at the door. She also had a remote-
controlled device that would allow her to unlock the door from
a safe distance, and a panic button she could press that would
call the police to her home in an emergency.

Marie and her husband received their patent for the home
security system in 1969. *The New York Times* reported on
the invention, and Marie won an award from the National
Scientists Committee. She died in 1999.

M is for Marie

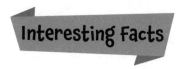

Interesting Facts

Modern home security systems
Homes with security systems are 300 percent less likely to be broken into than homes without security systems. Of homes that are broken into, those with security systems have an average of about three thousand dollars' worth of property stolen. Without security systems, thieves get away with about five thousand dollars' worth of property.

Queens, New York
Queens is the largest of New York City's boroughs. If it were a city of its own, Queens would be the fifth largest city in the United States. More languages are spoken in Queens than anywhere on the planet! It is home to the Mets baseball team, and to both John F. Kennedy and LaGuardia Airports.

Emergency calls
Fire departments pushed for the creation of a central emergency telephone number that could easily be reached from anywhere and would call out a fire crew in case of an emergency. The first known national emergency number was 999 in the United Kingdom in 1937–1938. In the United States, the first 911 phone call was made from Haleyville, Alabama, in 1968. Today, you can reach an emergency number by dialing 911 in 98 percent of North America, including the United States, Canada, and Mexico.

The New York Times

The New York Times is a daily newspaper produced and headquartered in New York City. It was founded in 1851. It is the eighteenth most-read newspaper in the world by circulation. *The New York Times* regularly runs articles on Black history and has a special project called "The 1619 Project" dedicated to the history of Black people in the United States.

Norbert Rillieux

Norbert Rillieux was a Black inventor and chemical engineer. He was born in 1806 in **New Orleans, Louisiana**. His father was a wealthy **Louisiana Creole** plantation owner, and his mother was a free Black woman. Even before the **one-drop rule** became a legal classification system, anyone with one Black ancestor (going back even several generations) was considered Black; one drop of Black blood made you Black, even if by appearances and culture you considered yourself a different race, like white or Indian. Because Norbert's mother was a Black woman, he was considered Black.

> ## Words You Should Know
>
> » **Chemical engineer:** A chemical engineer manufactures different products through chemical processes.

Because Norbert was from a wealthy Creole family, he had access to privileges other Black people did not have, like **education**. He attended private Catholic schools in Louisiana before leaving the United States to **study in Paris** at École Centrale Paris, one of the best engineering schools in France. Norbert studied engineering, physics, and mechanics and became an expert on steam engines. He taught applied mechanics at École Centrale at the age of twenty-four, making him the youngest professor to teach there up to that point.

While in France, Norbert started researching ways to make **sugar** production safer. Up until then, sugar had to be evaporated through a process of boiling the caned juice. Many of the slaves who worked in sugar mills suffered burns from the boiling liquid. He returned to Louisiana in the 1840s to oversee the installation of his machines at sugar mills there. In 1843, he patented his sugar refining machine which used a vacuum chamber to lower the heat needed to boil the sugar and eliminated the need for slave labor to transfer the boiling liquid into smaller pots. The machine was a big success, and many sugar plantations began using it to process their sugar.

Norbert returned to France in the late 1850s, where he lived until his death. It is possible that race relations were the reason he moved back to France. The Civil War was about to start, and **race relations** in the United States were changing so that even **free Black men** like Norbert were discriminated against. One of his patents was rejected in the US because it was believed he was a slave and therefore not a citizen of the United States. This made him angry.

In addition to the sugar **evaporator**, Norbert studied **Egyptian hieroglyphics** and built a similar evaporator for use with sugar beets instead of sugarcane.

He died in 1894.

Words You Should Know

» **Evaporator**: An evaporator is a device that is used to turn a liquid, such as water, into a gas or vapor.

» **Egyptian hieroglyphics**: Egyptian hieroglyphics were the system of writing that people in ancient Egypt used. Instead of letters, like our alphabet, ancient Egyptians wrote in picture symbols.

N is for Norbert

Interesting facts

New Orleans, Louisiana

New Orleans is the most populous city in Louisiana. It is located on a port on the Gulf of Mexico and was founded in 1718 by French colonists. New Orleans is known as a center of jazz music, for its Cajun and Creole cuisines and dialects, and for its big annual Mardi Gras celebration.

Louisiana Creole

Louisiana Creoles are people who are descended from the inhabitants of colonial Louisiana under both French and Spanish rule. The word Creole has nothing to do with race, and Creoles can be white, Black, or mixed. Many of them speak a distinctive dialect known as Creole.

One-drop rule

The one-drop rule became prominent in the early twentieth century under Jim Crow laws that forced separation of the races. If you had even one drop of Black blood, you were considered Black and had to follow rules and attend separate places, like separate schools, churches, hotels, bathrooms, lunch counters, and other day-to-day places and activities. Prior to the Civil War, one-drop rule also meant that many mixed-race people were kept in slavery even if one of their parents or grandparents was white.

Education of Black folks

Education has been an issue for Black people in America since they started arriving from Africa. Under slavery, Black people were not allowed to learn to read nor write, and, after slavery, Black schools didn't receive as much money as white schools to operate under Jim Crow laws that kept the school system segregated. Black teachers were less likely to receive training and education than white teachers, and Black students were more likely to drop out of school. There are still problems with racism in the public school system in America. Black students are more likely to be suspended from school or arrested on school grounds. Black students with disabilities are less likely to get the extra help they need. And Black teachers are still less likely to receive equal pay to white teachers for doing the same job. Schools in Black neighborhoods tend to receive less money for operations than schools in white neighborhoods. All this leads to more Black students dropping out of high school and less Black students going on to earn a four-year degree at a college or university today.

Black Americans in Paris

Paris, France, has long been a popular city for Black Americans. There is a long history of Black Americans moving to Paris to further their education and to live. Starting in pre-Civil War America, Louisiana Creole Black people and mixed-race people would send their children to Paris for college educations. Many stayed and lived in the city because there were fewer racial problems and they felt freer than they did in the United States where Jim Crow Laws enforced segregation. During World Wars I and II, many Black soldiers were stationed in France or went to Paris on break from the war. Jazz was popular in the city, and many Black musicians would go to Paris and perform and then stay there once they saw how they were treated equally to whites in the city. Many Black writers like James Baldwin,

Richard Wright, and Langston Hughes also traveled or moved to Paris and other parts of France because they were not discriminated against as they were in the United States.

Sugar

Until Christopher Columbus brought sugarcane stalks with him on one of his voyages to the New World, sugar was a luxury item that only the very wealthy could afford. Sugar is difficult to process and farming sugarcane is a dangerous job that requires a lot of backbreaking labor, so it was not a very common item. Once the trans-Atlantic slave trade started, sugar became a booming business. Known as "white gold," it was farmed throughout the Southern United States and Caribbean by Black slaves who had no choice but to work the sugar plantations. It was a very dangerous job. Sugarcane must be ground to a pulp, and many slaves suffered injuries from the grinding wheels or burns from the boiling process, in addition to cuts from working in the fields with large knives used to cut the cane stalks. Louisiana led the United States in sugar production and in the slave labor needed to produce enough sugar to satisfy the demand for sugar around the world. More money was made in sugar farming than in cotton farming, the second most profitable crop in the pre-Civil War South. Too much sugar in a diet can lead to obesity, diabetes, and cancer, and Black people are more likely to suffer from all three of these conditions today due to the amount of sugar in the modern diet.

Race relations

Race relations are the way different races interact with each other in society. In the United States, for most of its history, race relations have been poor, especially between Black people and whites. Prior to the Civil War and throughout most of the twentieth century, Black people have been discriminated against and, worse, even brutally attacked or killed, especially for speaking out about their rights. Despite the repeal of Jim Crow Laws, race relations in the United States are still stressed in many ways. Black people are still more likely to be injured or killed by violence than any other race in the country.

Free Black men

Free Black men, like Norbert, had more rights than slaves, but fewer rights than white people. They could travel freely, but, in many places in the United States, they had to carry papers that proved they were free. They were still subject to discrimination and Jim Crow Laws and had to stay in separate places from white people most of the time, but nobody owned them. They could choose what career they worked in and make ordinary decisions about their lives, unlike slaves who were forced to do whatever their owners chose for them.

Osbourn Dorsey

Osbourn Dorsey was an American inventor who designed a small thing that changed the world. Not much is known about his life, aside from the fact that he was born a slave in 1862. Although he was born into slavery, he was freed when he was just eight months old. Where he grew up is not known, but he obviously had a very creative mind because in 1878, when he was just sixteen years old, he designed and obtained a patent for a doorknob and a doorstop. Until then, **doors** could only be pushed open and pulled closed—there was no mechanism to turn the knob which allowed them to click into the frame. If one wanted to keep a door closed, it would have had to be held in place and locked.

Most of the information we have about Osbourn and his inventions comes from his patent applications. But in researching him, you'll run into many other important Black inventors, including Alexander Miles, who invented the elevator a few years before Osbourn invented the doorknob. In 1923, Garrett Morgan invented the traffic light. Inventor Fredrick M. Jones invented the thermostatic control in 1960.

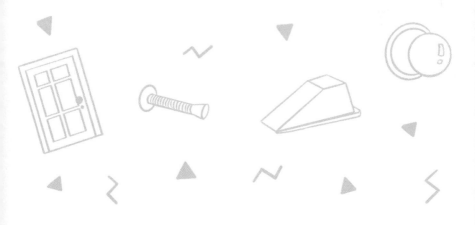

O is for Osbourn

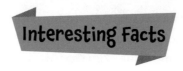

Interesting Facts

A brief history of doors

The earliest recorded doors date back to ancient Egypt, and were made of wood. They were single or double doors that hung pretty much the same way our doors are hung today: on a hinge that pivots to open. We don't have any of the doors from Egypt today, but they were painted in the tombs of pyramids, and some people believed they led to the afterlife. The oldest door that archaeologists have found is from Switzerland and is five thousand years old. The Greek scholar Heron of Alexandria (in Egypt) created the first automatic door in the first century CE. The first foot-activated sensor door was invented in China during the reign of Emperor Yang of Sui (614–618). He had the door installed in his library. The first automatic gates were invented in 1206 CE by the Arab inventor Ismail al-Jazari. Doors were often decorated with different metals and even jewels to show the wealth of the people occupying the building.

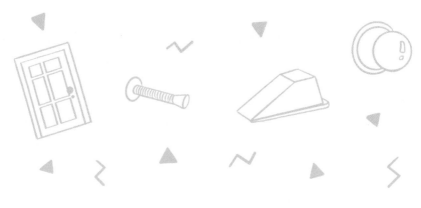

Philip Emeagwali

*"The hardships that I encountered in the past
will help me succeed in the future."*

Philip Emeagwali is a Nigerian computer scientist known for his work in **supercomputing** (using a large-capacity computer processor to analyze huge amounts of data). He was born in Akure, **Nigeria**, in 1954. He had to drop out of school at the age of fourteen because his father could not afford his school fees. Nigeria was in the middle of a civil war during Philip's childhood and he lived in a crumbling building. But he didn't let dropping out of school stop him from learning. His father continued teaching him at home, and he spent his days at the public library reading and studying mathematics, chemistry, physics, and English. He took a General Equivalency Degree exam from the University of London and then began applying to colleges in both the United States and Europe.

Words You Should Know

» **Supercomputer:** A supercomputer is a very powerful mainframe computer.

» **Environmental engineering:** Environmental engineers work to protect people from the negative effects of environmental inequality, including pollution. They also work to improve the environment to make it safer and healthier.

At the age of seventeen, he received a full scholarship to **Oregon State University**. He earned a bachelor's degree in mathematics in 1977 and went on to **George Washington University**, where he earned a master's degree in environmental engineering. He then earned a second master's degree from the **University of Maryland** in 1981. Philip loved learning so much that having two master's degrees wasn't enough: he earned a third master's in ocean, coastal, and marine engineering from George Washington University! In 1987, he was accepted into the civil engineering doctoral program at the University of Michigan. While there, Philip learned more about how oil is drilled. The country he is from is an oil-rich nation, which made him want to know as much as he could about the prices.

Philip set up a computer system using thousands of **microprocessors** to try to determine where oil reservoirs

Words You Should Know

» **Ocean, coastal, and marine engineering**: Ocean, coastal, and marine engineers build and test instruments and equipment that can be used offshore and along the coastline. Coastal engineers have to deal with rising sea levels, so they work to make sure that our coastal ecosystems do not erode and that the equipment they build can work in those environments.

» **Civil engineering**: Civil engineers build and maintain roads, bridges, dams, and similar structures.

» **Microprocessor**: A microprocessor is a circuit that contains all the functions of a central processing unit for a computer.

are located to make drilling more effective. As a result of his experiments, he discovered a way to make computers all over the world talk to each other. He is often called one of the fathers of the internet. Philip won the Institute of Electronics and Electrical Engineers Gordon Prize in 1989. Since then, he has won more than a hundred prizes for his work in supercomputing, and Apple computers used his technology in their Power Mac G4 models. He lives in Washington with his wife and son.

P is for Philip

Interesting Facts

Nigeria
Nigeria is a West African country. It has the seventh largest population in the world and the third largest youth population—nearly half of its people are under the age of eighteen. They speak five hundred languages in Nigeria! With all those languages, they need a common language to make communicating easier, so English is the official language. Nigeria was a British colony from 1800 to 1960, when they declared independence.

Oregon State University
Oregon State University had several protests led by its Black Student Union in the late 1960s and early 1970s. The Black Student Union threatened to leave the university due to discrimination, but the university worked hard to keep its Black students and opened a cultural center for them in 1975. Today, the Lonnie B. Harris Cultural Center serves Black students and makes sure their rights are respected at Oregon State University.

George Washington University
George Washington University was founded in 1821. During the Civil War, many of the students at George Washington University left the school to join the Confederate Army. The school was converted into a Union military hospital and treated injured soldiers on its campus. It is the largest college in the District of Columbia.

University of Maryland

During the Civil War, Confederate forces raided the University of Maryland campus. They were led by Brigadier General Bradley Tyler Johnson. The war was hard on the University of Maryland (then known as the Maryland Agricultural College). It lost a lot of money and had to sell two hundred acres of land. For a couple of years, the college closed down and became a boy's preparatory school. It reopened in 1867 with just eleven students. Today, the university has more than 41,000 students from all 50 states and 123 countries, and has over 200 degree-granting programs!

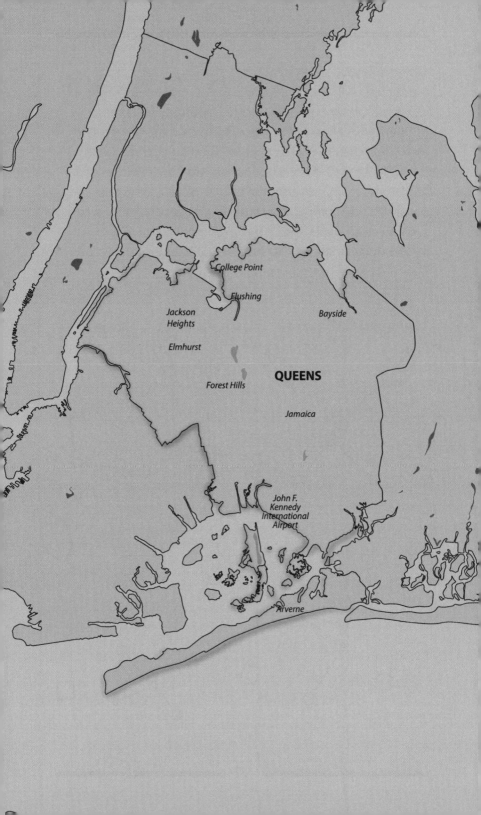

Q is for Queens, New York

Queens is the largest of New York City's boroughs. If it were a city of its own, Queens would be the fifth largest city in the United States. More languages are spoken in Queens than anywhere on the planet! It is home to the Mets baseball team, and to both John F. Kennedy and LaGuardia Airports.

Inventor Marie Van Brittan Brown was born in Queens. She invented the home security system along with her husband, Albert Brown.

In the Flushing neighborhood of Queens, you can visit the Lewis Latimer House Museum. Lewis helped invent the incandescent lightbulb, among other inventions. The museum features historical artifacts and information about his life and home.

Robert Henry Lawrence Jr.

Robert Henry Lawrence Jr. was an officer for the **US Air Force** and the first **Black American astronaut**. He was born in Chicago, Illinois, in 1935. Robert graduated from high school at the age of sixteen and earned his bachelor's degree in chemistry from **Bradley University** at the age of twenty. While in college, he joined the **ROTC** and did so well that he was made a Second Lieutenant in the Air Force Reserve Program. In 1956, he completed pilot training at Madden Air Force Base and was made a US Air Force pilot. By the age of twenty-five, he was teaching pilots in a program with the German Air Force. He went on to earn a PhD in physical chemistry from Ohio State University in 1965.

The Air Force selected Robert to test the Lockheed F-104 Starfighter, which was a big part of developing the Space Shuttle. In June of 1967, Robert was chosen to be an astronaut in the Manned Orbital Laboratory, making him the first Black American astronaut selected for space travel. Just six months after traveling to space, Robert died in a plane crash while instructing a student pilot. He was awarded a **Purple Heart**. In 1997, his name was added to the Space Mirror Memorial at **Kennedy Space Center** in Florida, a memorial dedicated to honor astronauts who have died in space missions or while training for missions.

Words You Should Know

» **ROTC:** The Reserve Officers Training Corps is a university training program for students that prepares them for military service.

» **Purple Heart:** The Purple Heart is a medal given to those who are killed or wounded in military action.

R is for Robert

Interesting Facts

Blacks in the US Air Force

The Tuskegee Airmen were the first Black military pilots in
the US Army Air Corps, which later became the US Air Force.
They trained at the Tuskegee Army Airfield in Alabama.
During World War II, they flew more than 15,000 missions in
Europe and North Africa. They flew so well that they earned
more than 150 Distinguished Flying Crosses! Prior to the war,
Black people were discouraged and sometimes prevented
from obtaining pilot licenses, because it was believed that
they could not learn to operate planes. The Tuskegee Airmen
changed that and helped lead the way to integration of the
Armed Forces.

Black American astronauts

There have been more than twenty Black American astronauts,
including: Guion Bluford, the first Black American in space;
Ronald McNair, who died when the Space Shuttle Challenger
exploded on reentry; Frederick D. Gregory, the first Black
American to command a Space Shuttle mission, and acting
administrator of NASA in 2005; Charles Bolden, administrator
of NASA from 2009–2017; Mae Jemison, the first Black American
woman to go to space; and Bernard Harris, the first Black
American to walk in space.

Bradley University

Bradley University is a private college located in Peoria, Illinois. There are over a hundred undergraduate and thirty graduate programs at Bradley. It was founded in 1897 by Lydia Moss Bradley, who opened the school in memory of her husband Tobias and their six children, who all died unexpectedly young. Today, Bradley University has over five thousand students.

Kennedy Space Center

Kennedy Space Center is located on Merritt Island on the east coast of Florida. Since 1968, it has been the most used of NASA's ten field sites for human space flights. The Apollo, Skylab, and Space Shuttle missions were all managed from the Kennedy Space Center. The Kennedy Space Center is now open to the public, and you can go there to tour the facility and ride on simulations of space missions!

Shirley Ann Jackson

"Do not be limited by what others expect of you, but confidently reach for the stars."

Shirley Ann Jackson is an American physicist. She is the first Black American woman to earn a doctorate at **MIT**. She is also only the second Black American woman in the United States to earn a PhD in physics. Shirley was born in 1946 in Washington, DC. Her parents valued education and encouraged her to do well in school. Shirley was in accelerated programs in math and science in high school and graduated as her school's **valedictorian**. She began her studies at MIT in 1964, when there were fewer than twenty Black students at the school. She was the only one studying theoretical physics. As the only Black physics student, Shirley experienced a difficult time. She was rejected by study groups of white students because of her skin color and felt isolated. But she worked hard and earned her bachelor's degree in physics in 1968. While studying at MIT, she also did volunteer work at Boston City Hospital and tutored students at the Roxbury **YMCA**.

She decided to stay at MIT for her doctoral work, in part to encourage other Black students to study at MIT, too. She received her PhD in **nuclear physics** in 1973, becoming the

Words You Should Know

» **Valedictorian**: A valedictorian is the top student in their class in high school and/ or college. They have the highest grades out of any student in the entire school.

first Black American woman to earn a doctorate from MIT. She studied **subatomic particles** as part of her post-doctoral work in both the United States and in Europe. After several visiting positions at laboratories in the US and Europe, Shirley joined Bell Laboratories in the Theoretical Physics Research Department, where she studied materials used to make **semi-conductors**. She is on the Global Board of **The Nature Conservancy** where she works to help preserve nature.

In 1999, Shirley became the first Black person and first woman to become president of Rensselaer Polytechnic Institute, a prestigious university in upstate New York. She continues to work at Rensselaer and actively champions political and philanthropic causes.

Words You Should Know

- » **Nuclear Physics**: Nuclear physics is the study of the protons and neutrons that make up atoms, and the study of how atoms are constructed.

- » **Subatomic particles**: Subatomic particles are the protons, neutrons, and electrons that make up an atom. There are other subatomic particles as well, such as alpha and beta particles.

- » **Semi-conductors**: A semi-conductor is a material that can conduct electricity at a rate somewhere between a conductor (like metal) and an insulator (like glass).

S is for Shirley

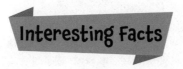

Interesting Facts

MIT

The Massachusetts Institute of Technology in Boston is a premiere research institution. It was founded in 1861 in Boston, Massachusetts. For many years, it was difficult for a Black person to get a degree at MIT, even though the school has always accepted students of all colors. Today, MIT has a diverse student population, and many Black students attend the school. MIT was directly involved with the founding of NASA and its space missions, and many of the people who worked on these projects are former Black MIT students. These include several astronauts!

YMCA

YMCA is short for the Young Men's Christian Association. It was founded in 1844 with the mission of helping members develop a healthy mind, body, and spirit. The YMCA is active in 120 countries and has 64 million members. They have physical exercise programs including swimming and basketball at most YMCA locations, and after-school programs for children.

The Nature Conservancy

The Nature Conservancy was founded in 1951 with the mission of preserving the land and waters that support life on the planet. They have more than one million members and over four hundred scientists on staff.

Thomas W. Stewart

Thomas W. Stewart was an American inventor with a very creative mind. He was born in **Kalamazoo, Michigan**, in 1823. He invented several things, but is best known for his **wringing mop**, a kind of mop with clamps and springs that allowed the mop to be wrung of excess water. He also made his mop head so that it could be unscrewed from the handle, allowing it to either be cleaned or discarded and replaced with a new mop head. He was one of the first Black Americans to receive a patent for his inventions. He and another inventor, William Edward Johnson, coinvented a **station and street indicator** that warned motorists of approaching trains. In 1893, he invented a metal binding machine that made it safer to bend steel.

Interesting Facts

Kalamazoo, Michigan

Kalamazoo is a city in the southwest region of Michigan. It was first settled in 1829. The name "Kalamazoo" comes from a Native American word thought to mean "boiling water," after the appearance of the Kalamazoo River. Today, Kalamazoo has a population of just over 74,000 people.

History of the mop

The oldest occurrence of the word "mop" was in 1496, but the word was spelled "mappe."

Station and street indicator

The station and street indicator that Thomas coinvented was an improvement over other station and street indicators and flipped a lever to show what street the railway vehicles or cars were passing. This was useful to show drivers where they were and what station they were approaching. It also warned people walking that a train or car was approaching so they could get out of the way.

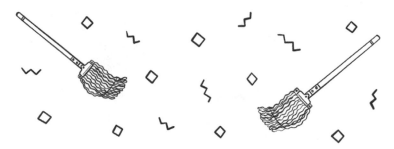

Valerie Thomas

Valerie Thomas is an American scientist and inventor. She was born in 1943 in Maryland. As a young girl, she became intrigued by technology while watching her father work on their television set. When her dad didn't encourage her interest, she began her electronics education herself at her local library. There, she found and checked out *The Boys' First Book on Electronics.*

Valerie went to an all-girls school where studying science and mathematics was not championed, but she didn't give up on her dream! In fact, when she went to college at Morgan State University, she majored in physics and then went on to work at the National Aeronautics and Space Administration, or **NASA**, as a data analyst. She became fascinated with an **illusion generator** she saw at a scientific exhibition and invented her own, using mirrors to project a three-dimensional illusion. It is a technology that NASA still uses today.

At NASA, Valerie worked to develop their satellite imaging program for "Landsat," a satellite that took images of Earth's resources from outer space. Valerie continued to work for NASA until her retirement in 1995. While there, she conducted research

Words You Should Know

» **Ozone layer**: The ozone layer is a protective layer of gas that surrounds the Earth's atmosphere and helps to absorb dangerous radiation from the sun.

» **Supernova**: When a star is getting ready to die out, it greatly increases in size and brightness, and eventually explodes. That is a supernova.

related to **Halley's Comet**, the **ozone layer**, and **supernovas**. She received a number of awards from NASA, including the Goddard Space Flight Center Award of Merit, and the NASA Equal Opportunity Medal. She continues to mentor young students through various programs today.

V is for Valerie

Interesting Facts

NASA

NASA is short for the National Aeronautics and Space Administration. It is an agency that studies outer space and aeronautics, and is responsible for the US space program. NASA used to be called NACA, which was an agency that was responsible for aircraft research, but when people began to dream of going into outer space, they changed their name and the focus of their program. NASA is responsible for the Apollo moon landing (the first time men set foot on the moon), the Skylab Space Station, and the Space Shuttle. They help the International Space Station with its mission, and are currently developing the Orion spacecraft and other programs.

Illusion generator

Valerie received a patent for a 3D illusion transmitter in 1980. The device produces optical illusion images by using two concaves, or curved, mirrors. Before Valerie's invention, flat mirrors were used to transmit illusions, but the images would appear to be inside or behind the mirrors instead of outside or in front of the mirrors. NASA first used the technology, but it has been adapted for use in surgery, as well as in video and television screen production.

Halley's Comet

Halley's Comet is a comet that appears in the sky about once every seventy-five years. The last time it was close to Earth was 1986. It is expected to return to Earth in 2061.

Pasi William Sachiti

Pasi William Sachiti is a **Zimbabwean**-born British inventor and entrepreneur. He was born in 1985 in Harare, Zimbabwe, and moved to the **United Kingdom** at the age of seventeen. When he was nineteen, he started his first business: an **internet** domain registration site called 123-Registration. In 2015, he went to Aberystwyth University in Wales, where he studied **artificial intelligence** and **robotics**. While still in college, he invented the world's first artificially intelligent librarian, Hugh. The robot could hold a conversation and direct students to one of several million books in the library. While studying at the university, William took an interest in technology that would allow for a driverless delivery service, and invented Kar-go, Europe's first street-legal, **self-driving car**. He continues to work on new inventions like "Trees of Knowledge," an invention that improves access to education for African children by making trees into educational hubs of information.

Words You Should Know

» **Artificial intelligence**: Artificial intelligence is the theory and development of computer systems that can do things like translate languages, recognize speech, and make decisions that usually require a human.

» **Robotics**: Robotics is the field of study dedicated to developing, designing, and using machines to do jobs humans would normally do. Robots are useful because they can do things that are too dangerous for humans to do.

W is for William

Interesting Facts

Zimbabwe
Zimbabwe is a Southern African nation that is landlocked. It used to be called Rhodesia, and was a British colony from the 1880s until it declared its independence in 1965. The people of Zimbabwe speak sixteen languages!

United Kingdom
Today, the United Kingdom is made up of four countries: England, Scotland, Wales, and Northern Ireland. During colonial times, the United Kingdom had colonies all over the world including North America, the Caribbean, and Africa. It was said that "the sun never set on the United Kingdom," because its colonies were all over the globe. The capital city of the United Kingdom is London. Slavery was legal in the United Kingdom until about 1800.

The Internet (early days)
The first internet was called ARPAnet, or Advanced Research Projects Agency Network. It was built by the US Defense Department. The first message on the ARPAnet, "LOGIN," was sent from UCLA to Stanford University and crashed both computers, which were each the size of a small house. The technology continued to develop through the 1970s, when scientists Robert Kahn and Vinton Cerf developed new software that better allowed computers to communicate with one another. Then, in 1990, computer scientist Tim Berners-Lee invented the World Wide Web, which is still used by millions of people to access the internet.

Self-driving cars

A self-driving car is a vehicle that can sense its environment and drive safely with little to no human input. Self-driving cars can be used for personal transportation, long distance trucking, deliveries, and robotic taxis. Several projects to develop a fully self-driving commercial car are underway right now. Waymo became the first to offer robotaxis in Phoenix, Arizona, in 2020, and Tesla has said it will offer fully self-driving vehicles to private owners in 2021. The delivery company Nuro will start delivery service with self-driving cars in 2021.

Madam C.J. Walker

*"Don't sit down and wait for the opportunities
to come. Get up and make them!"*

Madam C.J. Walker was an American entrepreneur and the first Black female millionaire. She is known for her line of hair care products. She was born Sarah Breedlove in 1867, just outside of **Delta, Louisiana**. She was the youngest of six children, and the first to be born free after the Emancipation Proclamation. All of her brothers and her sister were born into slavery. Her mother died in 1872, and her father died a year later, making her an orphan by the age of seven. She went to live with her sister Louvenia

> **Words You Should Know**
>
> » **Emancipation Proclamation:** President Abraham Lincoln signed the Emancipation Proclamation on January 1, 1863. It freed all the slaves in the United States and the Confederacy

in Vicksburg, Mississippi. As a child, she worked as a domestic servant to help her family make ends meet. The only education she had was three months of literacy training at a church Sunday school.

She married her first husband, Moses McWilliams, when she was fourteen to get away from her abusive brother-in-law. She and her husband had one daughter. Her husband died in 1887 when she was twenty years old and her daughter was two. In 1888, she moved with her daughter to **St. Louis, Missouri**, to be close to three of her brothers. At the time, it was a common problem among Black women to have severe dandruff and scalp issues. Sarah herself suffered from baldness, probably because of a combination of issues, including a poor diet. Her brothers worked in a barbershop and she started learning about scalp care from them. She went on to work for an entrepreneur named Annie Malone, selling hair care products and eventually developing her own line.

In 1906, she married Charles Joseph Walker and became known as Madam C.J. Walker. That same year, she and her husband began a mail order service for her products, opened a beauty parlor, and began a training academy to teach beauticians the Walker method. At the height of her career, Madam C.J. Walker employed several thousand saleswomen. She had a very active advertising campaign and put her image on all of her products. In addition to her hair care business, Madam C.J. Walker taught Black women how to manage their money, build their own businesses, and become financially independent. She was active in several different political and civic organizations and was known for her charity to different causes. When she died in 1919, she was worth between $500,000 and $1 million, easily the **wealthiest Black woman in America**.

W is for Madam C.J. Walker

Interesting Facts

Delta, Louisiana
Delta, Louisiana, is a small village of about 239 people. It is the birthplace of Madam C.J. Walker, and one of twenty-six sites on the Louisiana African American Heritage Trail.

St. Louis, Missouri
St. Louis is the second largest city in Missouri. It was founded in 1764 and was acquired by the US from France in the Louisiana Purchase. Just over 300,000 people live in St. Louis. It is home to the St. Louis Zoo.

Wealthiest Black woman in America
The wealthiest Black woman in America today is Oprah Winfrey. She is worth 3.1 billion dollars!

Betty X.

"I wish you power that equals your intelligence and your strength. I wish you success that equals your talent and determination. And I wish you faith."

Betty X, also known as Betty Shabazz, was a nurse and freedom fighter. She was born in 1934, and was raised by **foster parents** in Detroit, Michigan. Her parents were able to protect her from racism in Detroit, so Betty grew up with no understanding of what racism was. After she graduated from high school, she went to the **Tuskegee Institute** in Alabama where she was studying to become a schoolteacher. As long as she stayed on campus, Betty didn't have to deal with racism, because the students at Tuskegee were all Black. But in the nearby town of Montgomery, where she sometimes went on weekends, Jim Crow laws were in effect, and she had to wait for all the white customers in stores to be served before she could get help. This upset Betty terribly!

In 1953, she decided to try nursing instead of teaching as a career path, and left Alabama for New York to study at the Brooklyn State College of Nursing. While she was studying for her nursing degree, she met **Malcom X**, who was a minister with the Nation of Islam, an African American political and religious movement; the movement's stated mission is to improve the spiritual, mental, social, and economic conditions of Black people.

Betty converted to Islam and married Malcolm X, who preached for an end to discrimination and prejudice against Black people. They had six daughters together.

In February of 1965, Malcolm X was shot and killed, and Betty was left to raise their six daughters on her own. She began speaking about equality for Black people and went back to school, where she earned a **EdD** in higher education and curriculum development. After she earned her degree, she became a professor at Medgar Evers College, where she taught health sciences and nursing courses. Medgar Evers College is a public college in the City University of New York school system. It is located in New York City. It was founded in 1970 and is named after Medgar Evers, a civil rights leader. The school offers associate and bachelor's degrees and has just over seven thousand students today.

Words You Should Know

» **EdD:** An EdD is short for Doctor of Education. It is an advanced degree that people earn to study teaching techniques.

For the rest of her life, Betty continued to speak publicly about equality for Black people. She died in 1997.

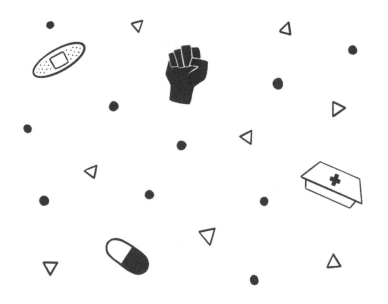

X is for Betty X

Interesting Facts

Foster parents

Foster parents are people who take in orphans and other children whose parents cannot take care of them. Sadly, non-white children, and Black children, in particular, are harder to place in adoptive homes.

Tuskegee Institute

Tuskegee Institute, now Tuskegee University, is a private, historically Black college located in Tuskegee, Alabama. It was founded in 1881. It began as a school for Black teachers under Booker T. Washington's leadership, and was home to the Tuskegee Airmen and scientist George Washington Carver. Today, it offers forty bachelor's degree programs, seventeen master's degree programs, a five-year degree program in architecture, four doctoral degree programs, and a Doctor of Veterinary Medicine degree. The university has about three thousand students from around the US and more than thirty countries.

Malcom X

Malcolm X was born Malcolm Little in 1925. He was a Black Muslim minister and preacher. He grew up in foster care like his wife, Betty X. He was sentenced to ten years in prison for breaking and entering in 1946, but while he was in prison, he met people from the Nation of Islam and converted to Islam. When he was paroled in 1952, he became one of the movement's most vocal ministers. He was popular during the Civil Rights Era and preached for equality between Black people and other races. He was assassinated in 1965.

Yvonne Clark

Yvonne Clark was an American engineer. She was the first woman to earn a bachelor's degree in **mechanical engineering** at Howard University, and the first Black woman to earn a master's in **engineering management** at **Vanderbilt University**. Yvonne was born in 1929 and raised in Louisville, Kentucky. Her father was a physician and her mother was a journalist. From a very early age, she liked to see how mechanical things worked. She enjoyed building things and fixing them. She was not allowed to take a mechanical drawing class in school because she was a girl, but in high school she was able to take an **aeronautics** course. She joined the school's Civil Air Patrol program, where she learned how to shoot a gun and took flight lessons in a simulator.

Yvonne graduated from high school at the age of sixteen and spent the next two years studying at Boston Latin School. She then went on to study engineering at Howard University, where she was the only woman in her class. She was not allowed to march at graduation with her male classmates. Instead, she received her diploma in the university president's office.

Words You Should Know

» **Mechanical engineering:** Mechanical engineering is the branch of engineering that deals with the design, construction, and use of machines.

» **Engineering management:** An engineering manager oversees engineering projects and ensures that they are run smoothly.

» **Aeronautics:** Aeronautics is the study of flight and design of aircrafts for flight

Yvonne had a difficult time finding a job after she graduated from Howard, because of her gender and because she was Black. She finally found a job with Frankford Arsenal Gauge Labs in Philadelphia, and later with RCA in Montclair, New Jersey. After marrying, Yvonne moved to **Nashville, Tennessee**, and was hired as an engineering professor at Tennessee State University, where she was the only woman professor in the engineering department. During summer breaks she worked a variety of engineering jobs, including weapons research at Frankford Arsenal, and designing containers to bring back lunar samples for NASA. She earned her master's degree at Vanderbilt University in 1972, becoming the first Black woman to earn a master's in engineering management. She won many awards for her teaching. Yvonne died in 2019.

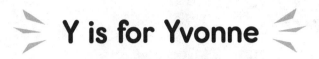

Y is for Yvonne

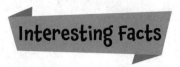

Interesting Facts

Vanderbilt University

Vanderbilt University is a private University located in Nashville, Tennessee. It was founded in 1873 and is named for Cornelius Vanderbilt, who gave the school the money to open. He hoped that by starting the university, he could help heal some of the wounds caused by the Civil War. Today, the school has more than 13,500 students from the United States and more than a hundred foreign countries.

Nashville, Tennessee

Nashville is the capital of Tennessee and its most populous city. It was founded in 1779. Nashville is home to a major part of the music industry and is also known as "Music City." It is home to at least six universities and is known as the "Athens of the South," due to the many colleges that are located there. About 690,000 people live in Nashville.

Zora Neale Hurston

"Those that don't got it, can't show it.
Those that got it, can't hide it."

Zora Neale Hurston was an American **anthropologist**, **folklorist**, filmmaker, and writer. An anthropologist is a type of scientist who studies humans, how they live, and their cultures. A folklorist writes down traditional stories from people in different areas of the world. Zora was born in Notasulga, Alabama, in 1891. She was the fifth of eight children in her family. All of her grandparents had been born slaves. Her father was a preacher and a **sharecropper**, and her mother was a schoolteacher.

Words You Should Know

» **Anthropologist**: An anthropologist is a scientist who studies human beings, their cultures, and their societies.

» **Folklorist**: A folklorist is a person who gathers folktales from different groups of people and records them so that they can be read.

When she was three years old, Zora and her family moved to **Eatonville, Florida**, which was one of the first all-Black townships in the United States. Growing up in an all-Black town meant that Zora didn't face any prejudice or see any limits to what she could accomplish in her lifetime. Her father even became the town's mayor! Zora's mother died in 1904, and her father remarried a woman that Zora did not get along with. They sent her to a boarding school, but she had to drop out when her father was unable to pay her tuition. She worked for a time as a personal maid to the lead singer of the Gilbert and Sullivan theatrical company. In 1917, she went back to school at **Morgan State University**, a historically Black college in Baltimore, Maryland, that had a high school on its campus. Zora had to lie about her age to get her diploma and told the school she was ten years younger than she really was.

After she received her high school diploma, she attended Howard University, where she started the school's newspaper and studied Greek, **Spanish**, English, and public speaking. She earned an associate's degree from Howard in 1921, and was then offered a scholarship to study at **Barnard College** of Columbia University, where she was the only Black student. While at Barnard, Zora's interest in anthropology was sparked and she studied cultures with several notable anthropologists and did field research in **ethnography**, or the study of culture. She studied anthropology as a graduate student at Columbia University for two years. While Zora was at Columbia, a movement of artists and writers was happening

> **Words You Should Know**
>
> » **Ethnography**: Ethnography is the branch of anthropology that studies different cultures.

nearby called the **Harlem Renaissance**. Zora became part of the Harlem Renaissance and spent her time with famous poets and writers like Langston Hughes. She also began publishing short stories. As part of her anthropological work, Zora traveled throughout the South and the Caribbean, studying culture and writing down folktales. She studied African American music and its tradition with slavery in Georgia and Florida with Allan Lomax, a well-known ethnomusicologist (someone who studies the music of different cultures). In 1936 and 1937, she traveled to **Haiti** and Jamaica and wrote a book about her studies there called *Tell My Horse*.

She also collected folktales for the Federal Writer's Project in Florida. And from 1947–1948, Zora lived in **Honduras**, where she hoped to find Mayan ruins, or the remnants of a lost civilization. The people in Honduras interested her because many had ancestors who had been African slaves. While she was conducting all this research on people and their cultures, Zora was also writing and publishing her novels, and even made a few films! She died in 1960, but there is still a festival held every year in her hometown of Eatonville that honors her work and her life.

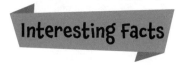
Sharecroppers

Sharecroppers are farmers who rent small plots of land from a landowner in return for a portion of their crop, which they give to the landowner at the end of each year. Sharecropping has been practiced all over the world for many centuries, but in the US, it was most common for former slaves to be sharecroppers.

Eatonville, Florida

Eatonville is a town in Orange County, Florida, just six miles north of Kissimmee. Founded in 1887, it was one of the first all-Black incorporated townships in North America. All-Black townships were often formed because the police refused to protect Black residents. Today, there are close to 2,400 residents in Eatonville. Every winter, the town holds the Zora Neale Hurston Festival for the Humanities. There is a Zora Neale Hurston Museum of Fine Arts in Eatonville, too.

Morgan State University

Morgan State University is a public, historically Black university in Baltimore, Maryland. It was founded in 1867. Morgan State in the largest of Maryland's historically Black universities. It has just over 7,700 students.

Black Hispanics

Most Black Hispanics in the United States come from Puerto Rico or the Dominican Republic, but they can also come from other places in the Caribbean and from countries in Central or South America, like Panama or Honduras. Black Hispanics are Black people whose first language is Spanish, or who come from Spanish-speaking roots. There are more than 1,234,000 Black Hispanics in the United States.

Barnard College

Barnard College is a private women's liberal arts college located in New York City. It was founded in 1889 because nearby Columbia University refused to admit women. Today, Barnard is affiliated with Columbia University, and students of Barnard can take courses at Columbia. There are about 2,600 undergraduates at Barnard.

Harlem Renaissance

The Harlem Renaissance was a revival of Black American culture and arts that was centered in Harlem in New York City in the 1920s and the 1930s. Fashion, arts, music, writing, dance, theater, and politics were all part of the Harlem Renaissance. The movement began after World War I, when many Black soldiers moved north to leave the South and Jim Crow laws. Harlem was the destination of choice for many of these soldiers. While the movement was centered in Harlem, it inspired a revival of Black culture all around the world, especially in Paris, France, where many Black artists moved to get away from the United States.

Haiti (and Black history)

Haiti is a Caribbean nation located on the island of Hispaniola. For many years, Haiti was a French slave colony, but from 1791–1804, the slaves and freed Blacks in Haiti launched a revolution. They defeated Napoleon Bonaparte's forces in 1804 and claimed their independence. Haiti is the only country in history to lead a successful slave rebellion and the first independent Black republic in the world!

Honduras

Honduras is a country in Central America. It was colonized by the Spanish during colonial rule in the sixteenth century. Honduras is home to many indigenous cultures such as the Maya, but also has a mix of Spanish and African cultures due to colonization and slave trade. Honduras declared its independence from Spain in 1821.